W9-CUW-803

Six Conversations For Getting
Organizations
Un-Stuck

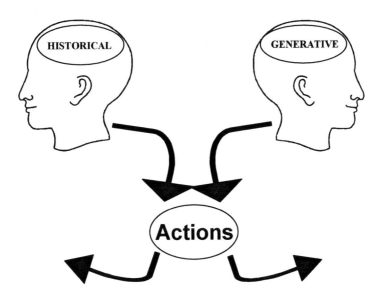

Life and work are accomplished through communication. Here are six conversations you must know!

By Mark Gladstone, MSOD

Six Conversations for Getting
Organizations
Un-Stuck

By Mark Gladstone, MSOD

Ron —
Thanks for all you've
contributed to my thinking
and understanding of consulting.
You are the genuine article.

— Mark

All Rights Reserved © 2004 by Mark W. Gladstone

No part of this book may be reproduced or transmitted in any form
or by any means, graphic, electronic or mechanical, including
photocopying, recording, taping or by any information storage
retrieval system, without written permission.

Acknowledgements

This work has been in mental outline form since 1998. Its completion six years later is a product of the encouragement and support I received from some very gracious people. So this effort is dedicated to them:

Dr. Stephen Schepman, David Lippes, Lara Hope, Terry Fleischman, Nathan, Wayne, Doris and Aubrey Gladstone for your reviews and comments. Thank you, your comments, questions and suggestions have added quality and readability to the ideas and concepts. And to my wife Sandra, for your unrelenting support, patience and editorial reviews. And more importantly for your proof of concepts, and for adopting with me the concepts of generative thinking and communication.

I stand on the shoulders of giants. Thank you Sam Magill, Dick Mayer and Paul Phillips for taking me under your wing. And to Dr. William Hitt, thank you Bill for your many works on leadership and the "Learning Organization". Your life was a model of personal excellence, and continues to be an influence on mine.

Table of Contents

Chapter   Page

    Introduction   6

1.   The Generative vs. Historical   10
    Mindset

2.   The Conversation for Results   24
    and Impacts

3.   The Conversation for Reality   42
    and Clarity

4.   The Conversation for Options   53
    and Alternatives

5.   The Conversation for   64
    Opportunities

6.   The Conversation for Initiative   68

7.   The Conversation for Closure   71

8.   Summary   79

9.   Application Assessment   83

Introduction

As an organizational development consultant I often get calls from companies that ask if I conduct organizational assessments or all-employee surveys. The conversation that follows typically goes something like this:

MG: We can, but first let me ask you, "How often do you like to do these surveys?"

Caller: We typically do them annually, or at least every other year.

MG: Do they typically show that you have poor communications?

Caller: Yes.

MG: Do they also indicate that you have low employee morale?

Caller: Why, yes.

MG: Do they also show that people would like more resources to do their jobs?

Caller: Uh, yes...what are you saying?

MG: Well let's wait on that for a second. Tell me, do you then establish committees or task forces to make recommendations to address these things?

Caller: Sure, that's pretty standard practice.

MG: So when you do the next survey, does it show that you have poor communications, low employee morale, and people want more resources to do their jobs?

Caller: Exactly...what are we doing wrong?

What is it that prevents organizations, or the otherwise intelligent and committed people from effectively dealing with their issues or problems? What I tell them is that they are in a historical "do-loop", a cycle or recurring pattern of actions or efforts that only serve to keep them stuck. They use the same thinking and historical solutions that helped create the current situation, hoping for a different outcome and impact. Each task force or committee is in effect putting different meat in the sausage maker, only to be disappointed when they continually get sausage. They are stuck. They are in the trap of trying to <u>fix</u> their existing organization, which only serves to re-establish and reinforce the organization they already have. If what they want is sleek, fast and modern transportation, and all they do is continue to keep fixing their same old clunker, then they are going to continue to drive a clunker. They are stuck. And at what a cost. Consider the following:

A 500-person organization conducts Quality of Work Life surveys every two years. The survey takes an average of 20 minutes to complete, 10 minutes to discuss, scoff, question, etc. with co-workers, and 60 minutes to review the tabulated results and findings several weeks later (estimates are conservative averages). The average fully burdened charge out rate is $50/hour. So we have: 500 people x $50 x 1.5 hours = $37,500. Then add the cost associated with having a group run the data and develop conclusions, the task forces or committee's brainstorming, drafting their proposed "fixes", communication and roll-out, and the direct costs (if any) of their suggestions. And when we add lost opportunity costs in to the mix, the figure could become staggering, AND they're doing it every two years and getting the same results.

So if fixing themselves (continuous improvement) is costly and not getting them the organizational change and results they want, what should they be doing instead? The alternative is simple, not easy, and profound. They could be generating or creating the organization they want, more and more everyday. This book is about creating and operating from a generative mindset, and with generative communications. Leaders who understand the generative mindset and its application don't simply improve their organizations; they transform and continually create their organizations, their relationships and sometimes, entire industries. The following pages offer specific guidance on how to use the Six Conversations to generate or create the outcomes you want for your organization, and get it unstuck. Creating the organization is not an end-point. It is an ongoing, unending endeavor.

How do you know when you are stuck? You keep getting the same results, revisiting the same conversations, bringing up the same old issues, and maybe feeling immobilized, not knowing what to do. Even a seasoned manager faced with a welcomed project, a new responsibility, or a favorable shift in the market can feel overwhelmed, and stuck. You know you or your organization may be getting stuck when you begin to observe:

- Stress increasing and remaining unalleviated;

- People expressing anger and frustration;

- People exhibiting low morale, depression, hopelessness, resistance and defensiveness;

- Highly talented people sub-optimizing, and doing less than their potential;

- People opting out, giving up and quitting; and

- People settling and adopting undesirable coping mechanisms.

With regard to this last characteristic, I have observed that most people hired for a job are happy to get the job. They are enthused and motivated. They are ready to give the organization all they have to offer. Then they encounter some bumps in the road, some situations, personalities, decisions, bias and favoritism, that deflates and disappoints them. After bumping into these things a couple of times they may begin to conclude, "this is just the way it is to work for this organization." It may be disappointing, but they accept it and they settle for it. But in their disappointment they also must figure out how they are going to survive in "this kind" of organization. This is where people may become cynics, sarcastic challengers of leadership, or they may withdraw and isolate themselves, or they may simply sub-optimize, doing only what is required to just get by. They adopt whatever means they need to survive the day in the company, for which they have settled, coping with the organization with which they now find themselves stuck! The unbridled enthusiasm and motivation they possessed when they first took the job goes uncultivated by the company. Even those employees who are generally constructive can lose their vision and ambition as the limitations of existing systems, processes, and culture become apparent and convey a message that "What the company really wants of me is to function within and comply with the existing structure and systems."

So why is it so difficult for people to extricate themselves from systems, structures and cultures with which they are dissatisfied? Continuous improvement programs should certainly result in continued constructive change, making people increasingly satisfied. So what goes wrong? One foundational aspect of the problem lies in the historical mindset and the communications that flow from it.

Chapter 1
The Generative vs. Historical Mindset

The historical mindset draws from our past, what we know, what we have done, the tools we have used, and past experience. The historical mindset is also our default. Our physiology and psychological make-up naturally lead us to default to the historical. That is, we are able to be more efficient in our daily lives because we have an automatic default to the past, to the things we have done and learned before, to our prior experiences and history. This historical default is what helps us to be efficient when we are trying to go home at the end of the day. It helps us to be efficient when we shave, do our hair, put on makeup or solve a problem consistent with how we have solved it in the past. We use the same strokes or movements as we did yesterday, and everyday prior to that. The historical default can become so automatic that it is almost unconscious. When we are stuck on the side of the road with a flat tire, where do we go to look for the jack? If our prior experience has been to find the jack in the trunk, it will help us to be efficient if we immediately go and find the jack in the trunk. It will frustrate and perhaps perplex us if we go to the trunk and find that there is no jack, learning later that this particular rental has the jack under the back seat. When trying to solve a problem the first move in our thinking is to ask "how did we solve that in the past"? This historical person (Historical Harry) primarily speaks of what is wrong by referencing something from the past, or something that happened a minute or a month ago. And further, Harry continually uses his past approaches to try and create different outcomes. For example when Harry looks at the production report and sees that his company is not producing or shipping sufficient numbers of product to keep up with incoming orders, he thinks: "Guess we'd better put in more overtime."

I recently observed a man at a gas station. He had pulled up to get gas for a rented passenger van. I watched him as he searched around his driver-side door and seat for a gas-tank cover release. He searched his instrument panel. He got out and walked over to the gas cap cover on the side of the van. He attempted to pry it open but was hesitant to force anything, fearing he would have to pay for damage. He pulled out and read through the owner's manual, but failed to find the needed guidance. I asked him if he needed help, and he explained his situation. He said he had owned a van like this for years; so he knew there had to be a gas cap release switch somewhere. I searched too, to no avail. Finally he used my cell phone to call the rental company. The agent advised him to press on the edge of the gas cap cover, which he did, and the cover popped open. This is an example of the historical default in action, but in this case, not very helpful.

This historical default, in its capacity to create efficiency, also helps to ensure that we get results similar to or consistent with the results we obtained previously. So when we desire to replicate previous results, then the historical default is absolutely the way to go. A nice smooth shave, the same appearance, the same level of quality in a product or service is all products of the historical default. The historical default is pervasive, establishing and reinforcing the patterns in our thinking, our communications, behaviors and almost every other element of our being. As you read this text, there are historical references tiptoeing through your thinking, influencing your perception of what is useful and what is not. "I've heard or read this before." "This is inconsistent with something I read before, or with something I heard." References to the past.

In contrast, and critical to moving out of the mode of simply "fixing" your organization, and shifting to a mode of "creating" your organization requires the discipline to adopt the *generative mindset*. The *generative mindset* is the mindset that draws from our imagination and ideas, and helps us generate or create what we want. It is a product of a forward-looking, future-orientation. It not only is quick to envision a better future, but also then concerns itself with imagining future solutions, structures, systems, technologies, capabilities, behaviors, etc. In Generative George we have a leader who takes in data on the current operations, and then asks himself, "So what's missing?" What is it that we need to create or put in place to become more of the organization we are striving to become.

From a generative mindset we are speaking of how we want things to be an hour from now, or a day, or a week, or a year from now. And that is the point. While it may seem trivial to move from an historical orientation to a generative mindset, it is a subtle but profound difference. And the difference is revealed in our communications that change and will dictate the response and the results. The communications are very different when you compare someone who is speaking of the future and what is possible, from the person who is speaking of what is broken, what is wrong, or even what is missing, but then applying past approaches to try and fill the gap!

I will offer specific examples throughout this book of the difference this simple shift makes in the communications and the results that are created. For now, consider this example: if we are speaking of the kind of management team we want to be or have in the future, we need to identify traits, characteristics, capabilities and capacities that we will have to learn and develop as we become that management team. (The current traits, characteristics, capacities and capabilities have only served to help us become the management team we are today.) If we are talking about the mistakes or problems we are having as a management team, the conversation will likely identify things from the past (historical) that we must stop doing, and failings in our efforts. Conversely, the future-oriented conversation helps us to identify what we can create or generate. It helps us identify what is missing. Generative George says, *"I know we could be operating at a whole new level. I see a management team where there is engagement, support, strong communication and mutual accountability for the overall results—not simply our own respective areas. Our management team meetings could be engaging, energizing, collaborative and progressive."*

In contrast the historical conversation points us to problems we must fix. And our efforts to fix these problems will also draw from things we know or have learned in the past, which, when you think of it have only helped us create what we have today. So our likelihood of creating something altogether different is minimal at best. Historical Harry says, *"We're not making any progress. We've tried that before, and the Union just didn't buy it. Furthermore, when I proposed that to my Clients their response was pretty lack-luster. But if you guys want to pursue it I can form a task force to look into it."* If Harry leads that task force, it is probably assured that it will recycle old approaches and past practices to recreate the results with which it is presently struggling. The generative conversation of what we could be and "what's possible" has an entirely different energy and dynamic to it. Seems simple enough I suppose. But check it out for yourself. Listen to some of the conversations and efforts to solve problems and see if they default to the past.

There is a television program that shows teams pitted against one another, challenged to create something out of old junkyard debris and scrap equipment. In one episode they were tasked with building a vehicle capable of moving under its own motorized power. Imagine if one team was forced to fix an old burned-out vehicle, while the other team was allowed to create a vehicle.

Historical thinking gives rise to historical actions, and the actions and patterns play out to recreate the results we've created before. This explains in part why organizations, work groups and individuals find themselves repeatedly trying to address the same questions, issues and concerns, heading down the same paths and pursuing tried and true (historical) methods. And we do so again and again with an expectation of a different outcome. The management team that discusses its problems and failings is likely to set itself up for recreating itself in its present image. After all, didn't we try to improve ourselves last time? Did we not bring the best of our thinking and ideas to solve or address our problems last time? Or have we really been holding back the solution until now? Not likely.

The model on the following page presents two domains of our thinking, and the relationship to actions and results.

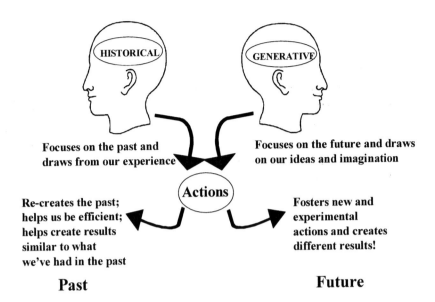

Focuses on the past and draws from our experience

Focuses on the future and draws on our ideas and imagination

Actions

Re-creates the past; helps us be efficient; helps create results similar to what we've had in the past

Fosters new and experimental actions and creates different results!

Past

Future

Shifting from the historical to the generative is one of those" simple-not-easy" concepts. We simply need to move from the "historical" domain of our thinking, to the "generative" domain. This is the domain where we generate or create ideas, where we use our imagination. Like the historical, the generative domain also gives rise to actions. However, because we are operating out of our imagination and new ideas, the actions generated are experimental and different, and best of all they create different results! We can then look at the new results, determine if they are in line with the type of management team or organization we are trying to become, and adjust or continue accordingly.

The historical default is what drives the battered wife home to the abusive husband. It is the refuge of the familiar and the certain, even if the familiar and certain run contrary to what we desire or are not in our own best interest. You may have experienced supervisors, managers and executives who have spent thousands of dollars in time and training to develop new tools and practices, only to return to that with which they are most comfortable.

Imagine how a work group might operate if from day 1 the people in that work group set out to create a high performance workgroup, examining breakdowns, quarrels and disconnects with a question of "How do we create a workgroup with the relationships, communication and alignment where that doesn't happen again?" "What's missing that we need to put in place?" "Since these occurrences are indicators that we are not yet the workgroup we desire to be, what do we need to do differently?" Everyday they could be <u>creating</u> something better. Organizations can do the same thing, and may attempt to do so through "Continuous Improvement" programs. However, if the basic mindset is not shifted from the historical to the generative, then a tremendous waste of effort and resources can result, old dynamics can recycle and the organization remains stuck with the same old problems. To create the organization that is desired and needed requires the generative mindset.

A vital component of the generative mindset is the ability to subordinate the ego for the sake of the desired future outcomes. Generative leaders understand this and exercise such ego management for the sake of their long-term goals. They have learned *that the ego doesn't care about your long-term objectives.* The ego doesn't care if you are number one in the market place, if you are the low-cost provider of choice, or if you have a great showing at the annual trade show. The ego just wants to be right, to win, to look good, to avoid embarrassment and loss, etc., in the immediate situation or conversation. It's not unlike coming home at the end of the day intending to have a nice relaxed, supportive, loving evening with your spouse. You walk in the door and are met with, "Hi Honey how was your day?" You begin to describe your day and eventually discuss an issue that arose at the office, and your spouse offers a suggestion or some alternative advice. The discussion subtly turns to debate, as you explain why "that approach" just wouldn't work. Your spouse persists in explaining why they believe it would work. Now the ego wants to win, to be right. And indeed, unless we have discussed the need and approach of subordinating our egos for our long-term, higher-level goals, both spouses' egos strive to win and be right. The longer-term objective of a nice evening has been pre-empted.

The management team goes to their annual offsite planning retreat. Among their business objectives, they also discuss ways they need to be operating. Historical Harry seems to be on board with the idea of mutual accountability for the division's overall results. Then the conversation turns to things his department needs to consider to assist the other departments. Harry's ego steps in and what we hear from Harry are defensive rebuttals and rationalizations as to why everything he is doing is the best that can be done. Harry is a rational person. He is a successful executive with a history of good accomplishments. He is committed to helping the organization succeed, and to do his best. Consequently, to suggest Harry is lacking in anything means that YOU don't understand what Harry is dealing with and why all of his very rational choices have been the right ones. By the end of this retreat we may well be headed back to "same ol' same ol". At the same time Harry's ego is intact!

You have probably heard people like Harry explain why this approach or that improvement idea just won't work. And the greater investment of ego someone has in the area being discussed, the more likely the ego will assert and pre-empt the longer-term objectives. Generative George understands this, and consequently exhibits a tremendous capacity to suppress his ego in the immediate situation, in deference to the longer-term goals. His ability to do this not only helps maintain progress toward their goals but also enhances his credibility with others. Historical Harry fends off alternative suggestions and push-backs with "I know what you're suggesting, Terry. But this organization just isn't ready to make that step. Our workforce just isn't that sophisticated. I already considered that option." (Ego wins, is right and appears so smart.) Generative George responds, "That's an interesting suggestion, Terry. It would require that we develop the computer skills of our workforce. And while I know we will eventually need to do that, my concern is whether we have the time and resources to do that this year. Help me think about how we could do that and still meet our commitments for this year." (Ego's need to be right is suppressed, openness and collaboration are fostered, and participation and involvement in the path forward are maintained.)

The ego wants:

- To be right
- To win
- To stay safe and secure
- To control
- To maintain
- To be first
- To look good
- To avoid embarrassment
- To validate its view of the world

And it wants all of these things in the immediate conversation or situation. Consequently, developing the self-awareness of when the ego is kicking into operation, and the self-discipline to subordinate the ego is vital to accomplishing your long-term objectives. When you subordinate the ego you tend to listen better (your defensive filters have been shut off) and you tend to seek new ideas and learning opportunities for how to do things differently to create a better outcome. Subordinating the ego is integral to the generative mindset.

Case File

Company XYZ is an organization with a history of over 35 years. It had been the target of several buy-outs and management changes. In the past it had not been especially profitable, but recently a multi-national conglomerate had bought the company with the obvious intent of turning the profit picture around. As a result the acquired organization began dealing with changes and challenges that included:

- Consolidation, integration and diversification of various operations with Corporate and other sites;
- Changes in reporting structures, including groups reporting to managers who were off-site;
- Loss of personnel, and their associated capacity, knowledge and experience;
- Regulator oversight, both audit findings and milestone commitments;
- Customer and quality issues, and the resulting "bad press";
- Heightened work pressure, longer hours, steeper production schedules, tight budgets, increased insurance and benefits costs, and changing performance expectations;
- A hazardous work environment with critical safety, containment and control requirements (people have to be alert and can't short-cut safety).

They were number 3 in an industry that was mature and offered no market expansion or new customers coming into the market. (Growth potential lay in taking market share from competitors.) The industry was highly regulated and quality critical. Their product was extremely price sensitive and their viability relied on keeping the price as low as possible. Their competitors viewed them as the most vulnerable player in this market, and their competitors' strategies appeared to be to push them out and shut them down. Their critical objectives were; how to meet the profit expectations of Corporate, expand market share, and avoid customer and regulatory issues? In January 2003, they were told by Corporate they had until the end of 2004 to turn a profit of $23 M. Their 2002 profit level was a negative $8.9M. They had only level operating budgets to work with, plus access to corporate reward resources.

The acquired division recognized it was going to have to do business differently and began to make investments to cultivate a "learning" culture, improve leadership and create a generative mindset for team operations and more open communications. After spending at least a quarter of a million dollars sending several hundred people through development workshops, training facilitators and establishing a team development process, Corporate intervened, sending new leadership to the division and charting a new path (that looked strangely familiar): Leadership development, training for teams and development of a culture that resembled that of the home office. However, since Corporate had a "historical" culture, it was unknowingly driving to establish a culture that reinforced and rewarded historical ways of doing things, self-interest and blind allegiance. The effect was to close communication channels. Staying quiet was staying safe. One senior manager for the acquired division even had compelling financial data that countered the reasoning of some significant corporate decisions. When asked if he was going to share the data, he explained that he had already shared it, and the decisions were made anyway. He was unwilling to bring it up again because he had seen other vocal managers "let go".

The acquiring organization not only stepped right into a historical "do-loop", but in doing so walked away from the investment they had just made. The above example is not unlike a farmer sowing seeds and waiting six weeks for a harvest that normally takes four months. Then when the harvest doesn't appear in several weeks, the farmer tills the field under and plants new seed.

What should the organization have done, rather than recycle through the same old approaches? In terms of generative thinking, they should have asked themselves: "What's missing at this point that we can put in place to help us move further and perhaps faster toward becoming the organization we must become?" "What can we put in place to accelerate our application and return on the training investment?" But in their case the historical default was too strong.

Assuming this idea of generative thinking makes sense so far, what guidance is useful in the practical application of the generative mindset? Because our thinking plays out in our communications, the application comes in the conversations we have with others and even our own self-talk: *those silent conversations that go on in our heads*. It is absolutely all about *our* conversations. *Our* conversations will either keep us stuck getting the same old results, or they will help us move forward. For example, look at the following statements. Can you tell which ones will tend to keep you stuck, and which ones leave open a possibility for moving forward?

- It's not worth asking. We just don't have the budget.
- We don't lose anything by asking.
- That's not the way we do things around here.
- Would you be willing to try something new, if it improved the work environment?
- I really need to get out of the house and do something, and I'd like you to come with me.
- You never want to go out and do anything.

- You guys are so negative.
- I want to be part of a group that's constructive.
- So how does a group like ours begin to try this?
- That may work for you, but it'll never work with this group.
- Why don't you ever help out?
- We're really going to need everyone's help on this. Can we count on you?

> **Some statements hold us back, while others leave us open to move forward**

- It's against policy, that's why.
- Who do we need to talk to, to get approval to try this?
- I'm not here to make people feel good or improve the work environment.
- I just want to do my work, but if I can help I will.
- You're asking people to give up a lot. That'll never fly.
- If this is going to work, we need to get Rex on board.
- Let's ask Rick if our assumptions are correct.
- You know what they're trying to do don't you?
- I guess I could quit.
- People just don't change, so I'm not about to.
- I don't know if it will do any good, but I'm willing to try.

Most of the above are pretty obvious. But "I guess I could quit" could be either generative or historical. That is, if your history has been to quit every time things get difficult, then quitting would be historical. It will only serve to take you down a path circling back to where you've been a dozen times before. If on the other hand you have felt shackled to the "golden handcuffs" of a corporate pension, then quitting might open up a whole new path forward, in which case it is generative. And that is the distinction. Some statements hold us back, while others leave us open to move forward toward what we want. The above examples are not meant to imply you need to dissect and analyze every statement you make. I have learned that attending to six conversations offers all of the structure needed to apply generative thinking. In the next several chapters we look at the Six Conversations for Getting Un-Stuck.

Getting un-stuck means we are able to make progress, get traction, and create different results. It requires attention to several different conversations:

- The Conversation for Results and Impacts;
- The Conversation for Reality and Clarity;
- The Conversation for Options and Alternatives;
- The Conversation for Opportunities;
- The Conversation for Initiative; and
- The Conversation for Closure.

Chapter 2
The Conversation For Results and Impacts

The *Conversation for Results and Impacts* concerns staying focused on the high-level results we are committed to creating, as well as the far-reaching impacts we want those results to foster. It means maintaining a continual frame of reference to that idealized end-point, vision or goal when in conversation with others, and even in one's own self-talk. And while the long-term results could be about the type of organization you want to create, or what market segment you want to dominate, etc., it could just as effectively be about the kind of strategic planning retreat you want to have next week, or other shorter-term goals. The beauty of this conversation is in how it brings people into alignment as to the "what" and "how". And it includes the following important elements:

1. Understanding the idealized results and impacts we want to create in the long term, and in which we all have a stake;
2. Creating mutual understanding among those with whom you're communicating regarding the importance of those results and impacts;
3. Translating questions, challenges, concerns and issues into values to create alignment with your results and impacts; and
4. Asking, "Who else" do you need aligned with you to ensure accomplishment of your results and impacts?

One would think that identifying the results and impacts is easy, obvious and simple to articulate. However consider how easily departments slip into parochialism and "stove-piping".

The Sales Department finds itself at odds with Production, who finds themselves at odds with Finance. And despite repeated messages from upper-management concerning goals and cost controls and production needs, the people in these various departments have lost sight of the higher level results to which they all are supposed to be working and in which they all have a stake!

Case Study

In one organization there was a Facilities and Operations (F&O) Department that had responsibility for facility operations and maintenance across a large research campus. The directorate had about 300 union members from about eleven different trades. It had specialists in Work Planning, Facilities Engineering, Environment, Safety and Health, Radiological Controls, and it had various layers of supervision and management. In total the directorate had about 600 people. The F&O Director recognized the old ways of doing business and providing support to the researchers were not going to work in an environment of declining budgets, reduced workforce and increasing regulation and oversight. Competing interests, in-fighting, avoiding responsibility, grievances and conflicts were eroding productivity and draining off resources. So she gathered her management team and her union stewards together for a conversation. She presented her assessment of how things were operating presently, and why the current mode was not going to be successful. She went on to explain the results F&O had to create and the impact it needed to have. She admitted she could not create the needed outcomes herself. She needed everyone in that room to be "on board" with her. She committed to doing whatever she needed to do to make the changes happen. Then she listened. She heard from her stewards, supervisors and managers. She heard doubt, skepticism, and all of the reasons why the current way of operating was just the way it was and why it was the best they could do. She heard where "we've tried that before and the Teamsters didn't..." or the "supervisors wouldn't..." or the "researchers weren't willing to ...", and so on. She heard resistance in the approach, but she reiterated the results that were critical to create. She did not argue for or defend the past efforts, she simply reiterated the impacts F&O needed to make. Her responses to their challenges and questions were similar to: "I don't know 'how' we'll do that as I stand here today. I only know we're going to find a way to make it happen. I don't care how we do it or who ends up doing it, but I know it is going to get done. If we're trying something and its not working, let's try something else, and tell me what you need from me. Remember it's not about the approach. Its about the results we create."

She maintained her focus on the results and what was at stake for everyone in the conversation. No one argued the merits of the results. The resistance came in the forms of self-doubt about the approach or the ability of the organization to overcome old patterns and ways of operating. The focal point became the results. Each pushback and voice of resistance was refocused on the results, and the group began to shift from doubts to results and then to possibilities.

Why? Why? Why?
I was called in to work with a client who was kicking off a significant culture change. As we discussed the desired results, he identified outcomes like better teamwork, greater flexibility, positive attitudes and reduced complaints. My challenge to him was "Why are these important?" With a slight look of surprise he thought for a moment and then said, "The absence of these things is costing us too much money.

26

We lose focus and waste time." "And why is that important?" I asked again. He paused for a moment longer and then said, "Well, if we don't optimize our operations and relationships and operate as a team, we lose our competitive edge, which means losing market-share and profits." When I asked a third time, "And why is that important?" he let out a sigh. After a moment's reflection, he offered, "Without profits and market-share we close the doors and go home. There go our livelihoods, mortgages and vacations." "Exactly," I responded, "so there isn't a single employee that doesn't have a stake in keeping this company viable and competitive."

When considering the conversation for results and impacts, ask yourself, "Why are these results important?" You will identify a greater need and outcome, in response to that question. But then ask yourself, "And why are those outcomes important?" Asking this question several times in succession drives you to some very high-level results that usually reflect the common stake that others will hold with you as well.

Why is it important to resolve the conflicts within our organization? Because dealing with conflicts distracts us from our work; draws resources off project to manage the conflicts; it creates stress and people do not work together as well. *And why are those things important?* Because in an environment of declining budgets and downsizing, we need to be getting the most of our potential, with a focused and cohesive workforce. *And why is that important?* It may offer the only true competitive advantage we have to maintain profitability and create a sustainable enterprise, and protect our respective livelihoods. It is clear that anyone and everyone in the organization is going to have a stake in helping the organization resolve its conflicts quickly and constructively.

When I am asked to facilitate large group meetings where participation involves differing interests or perspectives, I will frequently start the meeting with this ice-breaker: Silently at your tables, answer this question for yourselves, "Why is this work we are about to embark upon important? When you have your answer to that question, please stand up." I then wait until everyone is standing, and then I direct them to pair up with someone, and ask them that question: "Why is this work important?" I then tell them to listen to the response, and then ask, "And why is THAT important?" And then to ask the "Why is that important a third time. We then discuss the responses we heard, and it is quickly apparent that everyone in the room has a common stake in ensuring we conduct this work well, whether it is for the sake of a company, a program, an industry, or whatever. The commonality is vivid, and the results we are all committed to are understood.

Create Mutual Understanding of the Results and Impacts

For our Management Team to build the kind of organization we have envisioned, it requires that we have mutual under-standing of what we are talking about. To ensure that everyone is on the same page as to the results and

> **A great way for organizations to get stuck is for leadership to make pronouncements, and then assume everyone has interpreted the message exactly as it was intended.**

outcomes requires dialogue and management of the ego and defensiveness. (Remember, "dialogue" requires a shift from advocacy of positions to inquiry and seeking understanding, and helps us learn about the topic around which we are in dialogue.) To facilitate this outcome there are three questions to build the dialogue around:

1. What did you hear me say?
2. Where do you need additional clarity?

3. What's missing for you?

(These are not to be confused with those very familiar "parental" admonitions: "Now what did I just say? What don't you understand?")

When groups create the opportunity to discuss these three questions it ensures everyone leaves the conversation with a common understanding.

What did you hear me say? This question is focused on learning what was communicated to the audience. With responses to this first question, the leader knows what he or she has communicated. The initial speaker is afforded the opportunity to hear how the message was received, and then reiterate or emphasize key messages, to correct misinterpretations, and to fill in gaps.

Where do you need additional clarity? This question is focused on terms and phrases that are subject to subjective and widespread misinterpretation. When the one who spoke hears the responses to the second question, it allows everyone to have a common interpretation of ambiguous terms. For example, an employee might respond to the question with, "When you say 'zero-tolerance for quality defects' what's that mean in the practical sense? Because we all know we could commit a huge amount of time to produce perfect products, but the cost would be prohibitive." Someone else might ask. "What do you mean when you say 'cost cutting'? Are we talking about jobs?" The CEO has the opportunity to be explicit about what he means. The dialogue around this question is

> **The focus of the dialogue is to ensure everyone leaves the room with a common understanding of the results, goals and objectives we are committed to collectively creating.**

heard by everyone in the room and ensures no one leaves the room with a different interpretation than what was intended.

What's missing for you? Finally, responses to the third question help reveal parts of the path forward that might otherwise have been overlooked or not addressed. For example, someone might respond with "What's missing for me is how we're going to cut costs without cutting jobs." An honest response to that point allows everyone to deal with accurate information. In some cases the leader may respond, "We've made all of the cuts we're going to make. Now we have to determine how we can get our work done with the workforce that remains." Another situation might require this type of response: "That's a very valid point, and it is a challenge we will have to face. In reality we may have to cut some jobs. However, we'll attempt to address such cuts through attrition if at all possible." And so on. Another employee might offer that what's missing for him/her is "How are we going to meet the new audit requirements of the regulators?" To which the leader might respond, "That's a good point, and one we'll have to keep on our screen. Terry, would you be willing to help us think about how to work that into our efforts?"
That is the approach Generative George chooses to use.

If you have ever been tempted to give your "I have a vision" speech and you were not going to afford your audience the opportunity for this critical dialogue, save your breath. You don't get there by simply asking, "Are there any questions?" Consider the style of Historical Harry: he conveys his message, assumes there is complete understanding, asks, "Does anyone have any questions?" and then exits the room dusting his hands in satisfaction, "There, they've got it." At the same time however, exiting the room through the opposite doors some employees are expressing, "I don't get it. So what's changed?"

The focus of the dialogue is to ensure everyone leaves the room with a common understanding of the results, goals and objectives we are committed to collectively creating.

Translate Resistance, Issues and Concerns to Values

In the *Conversation for Results and Impacts* we must anticipate running into resistance and cynicism. The historical default will be at work. People may push back, expressing issues and concerns. This is where <u>it is vital for the leader to translate issues and concerns to the values they represent</u>. Consider the following examples. On the left side of the table below are several very common workplace issues. The values they may represent are translated on

> **The ability to translate issues and concerns to values may be the single most important tool for managing resistance.**

the right side of the table. To assist in this translation process I like to use the following prompt: "They want to be a part of an organization where...."

Issue or Complaint (The issues below reveal values in the right-hand column.)	Values (They want to create an organization where...)
Too much work not enough time	...workloads are shared equitably; ...they can do work of the highest quality; ...there's sufficient opportunity to think creatively about how they can do their work better; ...there's time to build effective working relationships; ...there is home and work-life balance;

Issue or Complaint (The issues below reveal values in the right-hand column.)	Values (They want to create an organization where...)
Negativity of coworkers	...they have constructive relationships; ...they encourage and build each other up; ...they work together to affect constructive change where they can; ...their work and work relationships build energy rather than drain it off;
Bureaucracy and steps that don't add value	...they commit their time and resources to doing the high-value work; ...they have processes that are logical, and add value; ...they make it easy to access the expertise, resources or decision makers with a minimum of hassle; ...they operate with a bias for progress and results;

Notice that the values underlying any particular issue are not simply stated as the opposite of the issue. That is, "negative co-workers" is not simply translated to "positive co-workers". There may be numerous factors of personal importance. People adept at translating concerns and issues to the values represented in those issues, find they encounter far less resistance, and enjoy greater engagement and better alignment of people to the results he or she wishes to create. They are asking themselves, "Why do they care about this issue? Why would I care about this issue? What have I desired when I have voiced such concerns?" This helps to identify the underlying values, and the value side of the equation is generative, future focused, and it usually depicts values that most people hold in common. Thus while the complaint or issue can separate us, even polarize us, the values bring us into alignment.

Case Study

A millwright working at a Government facility received his work assignments for the day. First on his list was the replacement of a filter in a large ventilation shaft that drew exhaust from the bench of one of the laboratories. The millwright was aware that some pretty nasty (radio-chemical) fumes and exhausts had been drawn through the shaft. Because he was concerned of the health risks, he asked for full coveralls and "fresh air" piped into his mask. The millwright's supervisor viewed the request as extreme and told him the work did not warrant such measures, which would also add time and cost to the work. The millwright argued his concerns, and the supervisor continued his resistance. The supervisor told the millwright that the Industrial Safety representative had already "signed-off" on the work, and provided a copy of the "Health Risk Assessment" to the millwright. The millwright could not make sufficient sense of the assessment to give him the confidence that his health would not be at risk. He continued to press the issue, and was told by the supervisor that if he didn't do the work as directed it would be considered insubordination and he would be sent home. At this particular facility, workers were provided a "Stop Work" card that they could display to stop work on any job where they felt there was a health or safety risk. The millwright pulled his card and demanded, "Stop Work!" The exasperated supervisor responded by calling in his manager. When the manager heard the supervisor's story he told the millwright to either get to work or go home. The millwright left, but he didn't go home. Instead, he went to the local Government Safety Concerns Office and filed a complaint. The complaint was investigated and the investigating office advised the millwright's management that the concern was valid, and they needed to work with the millwright to reconcile the issue.

It was at this point I was called in to facilitate the discussions between the millwright and the management team. Knowing that issues translate to values, I began by asking the millwright to again tell his story and explain what happened. As he told his story and voiced his issues I took notes. They were not notes of what he was saying, rather, they were my thoughts as to the values his issues represented. I jotted down what I thought he was saying about the kind of organization he wanted to work for. That is, I was writing down my version or interpretation of the values his concerns represented. When he finished his story, the three managers began rebutting and defending themselves and voicing blame toward the millwright. I asked for their attention and asked them to listen to what I had heard:

> What the millwright said was that he wants to be part of an organization where...
> ...the work can be completed safely;
> ...the perspective and experience of the worker is respected and utilized in identifying safety or health risks;
> ...there is a supportive supervisory and management team;
> ...the health risk assessments are easy to understand and the workers can have a high level of confidence in them.

I then asked the management team, "Which of those things do you <u>not</u> want or you disagree with?" They responded that they wanted all of those things. At which point we discussed how this whole episode and the millwright's concerns are simply evidence that as an organization they are not enough of those things, *yet*. And that was the point at which they let go of the finger pointing, blaming and defending (the historical), and shifted into the generative mode of creating more of the organization they wanted. They moved from resistance to creation and solution, and more into alignment around the results and impacts important to their organization.

The effect of working together to fill the gaps had a positive effect on the relationship between the millwright and his management. There was better understanding and greater respect for each other. It should also be noted that management did an admirable job of managing their egos, suppressing historical conclusions and moving to the creative mode.

Because issues and concerns are not always revealed in a facilitated session or explicit fashion, it may be helpful to look at how translating issues and resistance might occur in a typical exchange.

The diagram on the next page presents a theoretical example of a possible exchange.

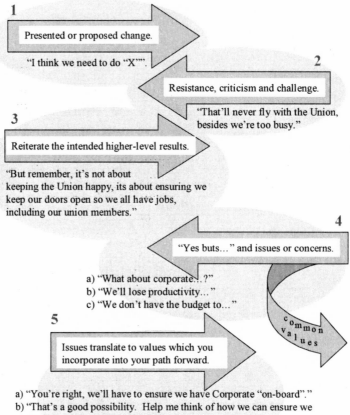

1 Presented or proposed change.

"I think we need to do "X"".

2 Resistance, criticism and challenge.

"That'll never fly with the Union, besides we're too busy."

3 Reiterate the intended higher-level results.

"But remember, it's not about keeping the Union happy, its about ensuring we keep our doors open so we all have jobs, including our union members."

4 "Yes buts…" and issues or concerns.

a) "What about corporate…?"
b) "We'll lose productivity…"
c) "We don't have the budget to…"

5 Issues translate to values which you incorporate into your path forward.

common values

a) "You're right, we'll have to ensure we have Corporate "on-board"."
b) "That's a good possibility. Help me think of how we can ensure we keep people productive and focused."
c) "So if we can find a way to do it with existing resources and minimize off-project time, can I count on your support?"

Translating resistance, issues and concerns to values is a vital part of the conversation for results and impacts. Generative people understand this, and practice this as a routine part of how they operate and communicate.

Tip: *Until you have developed your capacity to translate issues to values during a conversation, right in the moment, I recommend soliciting the issues explicitly. Then ask for some time to think about them, and translate them. Then reconvene with the person and have a discussion in which you say "I've thought about your issues and it sounds to me like you're saying..." Offer your interpretation of the values and move the resistance to finding ways to building their values into your proposal.*

Case Study

An Executive Director, whose agency provided living support to the developmentally challenged, was at the end of his rope in what to do about an abrasive and imposing guardian. The situation had developed to the point that the Director was ready to relinquish the contract. He contacted me to see if there was any way to salvage the relationship. I learned that the guardian (the father of the client in the agency's care) was frequently stopping in at the client's home and criticizing and accusing the agency staff of negligence and misconduct. He would make subtle threats and put the staff on edge.

I conducted interviews of the guardian and the staff members. The guardian said he was concerned that staff were not managing household funds correctly. He said his son is required to wear a mask at night for oxygen, but that staff were not complying. He said the staff were serving his son the same meals day after day, and not varying his diet. He also contended that his son was not participating in some of the activities in which the guardian wanted him involved.

The staff members complained that the guardian would come over to the house at any time, day or night, including after midnight. They said he was accusatory and bullying.

They also said his visits were a distraction for them (from the client's care) and distressful for the client. When I asked them about the oxygen mask, they explained the client was extremely uncomfortable wearing the mask, would get upset and not sleep well. When they asked the visiting nurse about it, she told them it was not required.

After the interviews, I examined their issues and concerns and identified the values reflected in those concerns. We convened the whole group (Director, staff and guardian), and I presented to them my interpretation of their issues:

"First and foremost, everyone in this room is unquestionably committed to the care and comfort of the client, and his quality of life. The guardian seeks <u>the best care</u>, with <u>variety in diet and activities</u>, and <u>efficient management of the household resources</u>. The staff desire to deliver the best care in an <u>environment of trust, confidence and support</u>. <u>Providing all required medical care, while minimizing discomfort for the client</u>. And to operate with <u>clear and unambiguous guidance</u> with regard to that medical care." I asked if anyone disagreed with anything they had heard from either side. No one disagreed. I explained that they were all in relationship as to the results and impacts they were trying to create for the client, and that their issues simply indicated they weren't quite "there" yet, or that they were not communicating sufficiently to keep everyone aware that they were "there".

There was further discussion on ways to improve communications and they set down some agreements as to visiting times, diet, and maintenance of household financial records. These ground rules were put into a simple assessment form, along with the values (underlined above). The group met on a monthly basis for the next three months. At each meeting they would take a moment to complete their assessment on how well they were executing on their values and agreements. They would then use the assessment to examine any "low" scores and discuss possible ways to bring the score up. In the end the contract was saved, the relationship was vastly improved, and the client's quality of care was increased. Issues to values.

Who else?

Finally, a vital part of creating the results and impacts we desire is the question of "Who else needs to be on board with us to ensure we accomplish these results successfully?" "Who poses a source of needed support, guidance, regulatory influence, or even resistance?" Then with those we have identified, we entertain the other elements of

> **Achievement of our desired results may require us to engage decision makers, opinion leaders, primary resistors, and those who will influence implementation or vital**

the *Conversation for Results and Impacts*:

- Presenting the high-level results and far-reaching impacts to which we are committed, and the importance of achieving those results (why...why...why?);
- Ensuring mutual understanding through dialogue around the three questions:
  1. What did you hear me say?
  2. Where do you need additional clarity?
  3. What's missing for you from what I said?
- Translating their issues or concerns to values that we probably hold in common; and then
- "Who else do we need to have on board?"

As unlikely as this next example sounds, it is true. One woman I met was a computer technician in an Information Systems Department for a county government. Their entire system had been down for several weeks. They had called in local computer consultants who tried everything they knew to do, to bring the system back up. The technician remembered someone had given her a phone number, telling her, "Here, try this. This is the number for IBM's CEO (Lou Gerstner)." She had considered it a joke two weeks ago. But now, she sought out the slip of paper and decided to give it a try, joke or no joke. She dialed the number, and was pleased to hear the receptionist's voice say, "Good morning, Mr. Gerstner's office." The technician explained their plight, and in response received a mini-tutorial on the maintenance agreement and support resources in the license agreement. The technician persisted, offering to fax the 17 pages of everything they had tried over the past three weeks. The voice on the other end asked, "Can you hold for one moment please?" After a brief hold-time, a senior executive responsible for customer service came on the line, introduced himself, and began asking the technician for the characteristics of the problem(s). Within days the system was back up and operating. For the next six weeks, the technician received periodic calls from the executive, asking her how things were operating.

"Who else?" Sometimes our answers to that question may seem far-fetched or preposterous, but if what we are striving for is important, then we have to bring those people on board with us to achieve our desired results.

In summary...
Organizations and people can get stuck if...
- They've lost focus on the higher-level results and impacts they're trying to create;

- They're rushing past the critical discussion that ensures they are mutual in their understanding of the situation, objectives, feelings and terms;
- They are seeing or hearing only the issues or concerns and they're not translating the issues to values; values with which we most likely agree; and
- They are not being deliberate in asking, "Who else needs to be on board with us as to the results and impacts?"

The *Conversation for Results and Impacts* is the conversation that raises our awareness to the important outputs of our efforts. By attending to this conversation we can let go of squabbles over the approach, and ensure alignment to the results. It moves us to a place where we can work together to create the results to which we are committed. I no longer require you to use my approach, because I know that you are committed to creating the same results, regardless of the approach you use. Our level of trust increases. We can use the issues and concerns of others to flesh-out additional details in how we need to go about achieving our results. And we can assure ourselves that we are bringing everyone on board who needs to be on board.

Once we have mastered the *Conversation for Results And Impacts*, we can reduce the greater percentage of resistance, conflict, and the delays in dealing with such resistance.

Chapter 3
The Conversation for Reality and Clarity

The second conversation that helps us to stay in a generative mode is the *Conversation for Reality and Clarity*. It is a conversation restricted to facts, data and objective observation. This means that in this conversation there are:

- **no opinions** about the way things are;
- **no assumptions** or conclusions about how the world works;
- **no attributions** of motives and intention of others; and
- **no self-conclusions** about 'just being the way I am.'

All of these elements, opinion, conclusions and attributions are based in history. It is by past experience that someone will offer, "Well you know culture change just doesn't "take" around here." "Anyone will tell you, there's just no way to eliminate the overtime problem." "You know what management is trying to do don't you? They're trying to pad their bonuses by cutting employee benefits." "You know what the Union is trying to do don't you?" Such assumptions, opinions and attributions have promoted the behaviors and communications that brought us to the present state, and only serve to keep us stuck with what we have. When people operate out of such conclusions, it limits their initiative, sense of possibilities and progress.

If we embark on a road trip from Seattle to Pensacola, we may plan to be in Pensacola in six days.

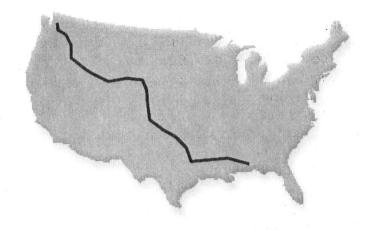

If six days later we find ourselves in Denver, we can ask, "Where should we be?" What would you say? Passengers on our bus might say, "We're supposed to be in Pensacola!" The disappointed passengers might go on to offer their opinions and conclusions: "This bus company doesn't know how to drive around the block. That driver is clueless! They should have their license pulled!" Employees commonly have such attributions and conclusions about their 'leadership'. How often are the problems of an organization attributed to the leadership? You may have only been promoted to management yesterday, but you are now considered part of the problem. But through the *Conversation for Reality and Clarity* we identify just the facts of what happened:

- We pulled out of Seattle on time but then ran into that snowstorm on the mountain pass, and the driver had to "chain up" and stop again to take off the chains;
- We made good time to Idaho but we ran into that construction and we were backed up for several hours.
- There was the detour out of Ogden…
- The pregnant lady going into labor…
- Etc.

So when we look at the facts of "what happened" and we ask ourselves "Where should we be?" the answer is always: Given what happened, it makes sense that we are where we are. Every organization is the way it is, has the culture and morale it has for all of the right reasons. But people harboring resentments from the past, and maintaining assumptions about others' intentions and motivations, prevent the organization from being able to move ahead and create the type of organization it desires to be.

Consider an organization where management feels there is mistrust between management and the general employee population. So management decides to conduct some focus groups to learn what issues are most bothersome to employees. It provides an opportunity for the organization to become more aware of what is causing or promoting the lack of trust, and how it might possibly improve itself. If an employee attributes ulterior motives to management, e.g., "Management is just trying to identify the nay-sayers so they can get rid of them!" then that employee and perhaps others with whom he has spoken withhold their input and feedback to management. Since management is not aware of the issues or experiences that have fostered the distrust in those employees, they have no way of addressing them. So the culture and environment of distrust remain intact.

However the *Conversation for Reality and Clarity* challenges us to simply stick with the facts:

> Two years ago Joe was told he'd be able to have a week off for vacation at fiscal year-end. (fact).
> When fiscal year-end came, two co-workers in Joe's group had left the group, and had not yet been replaced. Joe's group was short-handed. (fact).
> Joe's supervisor told Joe he needed him to work to help closeout the fiscal year, and forego his vacation plans. (fact).

Joe felt betrayed and concluded, "You can't trust anything management says!" (His conclusion and feelings are facts. It is how he felt and what he concluded.)

Now, Joe's manager said she wanted to address the distrust of management. (fact.)

Joe felt skeptical. (fact).

Joe's manager convened 6 focus groups to gather input. (fact).

If Joe sticks to the facts, reality and clarity, he can say, "Based on my experience I am skeptical as to whether anything will come of it, but *in the interest of generating or creating something better*, I will tell them what I have observed and encountered."   If Joe participates and conveys the facts of what he has experienced, then that is helpful. If on the other hand, Joe attributes motives to his supervisor, e.g., "She was just pandering to me, so I wouldn't take vacation earlier in the summer, and then when it came time for my requested vacation, she didn't think twice about just jerking me around!" Faced with such attributions, Joe's manager may get driven to defensiveness and rationalizing. This could then have the effect of polarizing the parties, and causing the focus group to breakdown. Let's take it a step further.   If management were frustrated that Joe "derailed" the focus group, that he maintains a bad attitude, attacks management and promotes dissention, then maybe they would decide to "deal" with these performance problems. In which case Joe can go back to his co-workers and say, "See, I told you management was just going to go after the 'nay-sayers'. I spoke out and now management is putting me on probation."

By staying with just the facts, and suspending our conclusions and assumptions, it brings us to the point that we are where we are for all of the right reasons, and leaves us open to possibilities and constructive change.

This is true for our internal conclusions as well. Consider this scenario:

Jill: Hey be sure to invite Finance to that program review.
Phil: I don't know. They've proposed to assume oversight over the Contracts Department. I think they're going for a power-play. And the last time I asked Tom for a delegation of authority, he put me off and I never did get an answer. I think they're viewing us as subservient.

The assumption and conclusion that the Contracts Department is the target of a "power-play" and is subservient prevents the Contracts Department from making a call that might otherwise result in a better program for the organization. It might also demonstrate trust, collegiality and collaboration that have been missing between the Finance and Contract groups.

Attributions
Consider a past customer or client who has failed to return your calls or e-mails. The temptation might be to conclude that they are no longer interested in doing business with you. If you attribute that motive to your client and operate from that conclusion you may refrain from making follow-up calls or contacts and you indeed lose the customer. It is more useful to stick with the facts, suspend any assumptions, and make another call. It may be the call where you learn about the client's daughter having undergone prolonged treatments, keeping your client away from the office, and unavailable to return calls. And it may also be the call where the client says, "Your timing is perfect. I just got back into the office and was thinking about who to call for help on a new project."

The *Conversation for Reality and Clarity* is in keeping with the thoughts of James Cozzens, who wrote in "Guard of Honor":

A great many people, maybe most people, confronted by a difficult situation, one in which they don't know what to do, get nowhere because they are so busy pointing out that the situation should be remade so they WILL know what to do...

There are reasons for every thing that is. They're often interesting. Figuring them out increases our understanding. They may arouse our indignation or our compassion. They add up to say that if things had been different, things might be different. That seems quite likely; but things aren't different, they are as they are. That's where we have to go on from."

It suggests that it is all very interesting to try and find out why something happened, perhaps even to assign blame. People become impassioned or upset. But it all adds up to say we are right here right now, so what do we want to do to generate and create what we want or need.

There is the story of the American woman traveling in Britain. As she waited at Heathrow Airport for her plane, she decided to buy a book to read and a box of cookies to snack on. She found a quiet table and sat down to read her book. Shortly thereafter an older British man asked if he could sit at her table and read his paper. She obliged him. Moments later looking up from her book she noticed he was taking a cookie from the box. She stared at him somewhat taken aback by his boldness. He smiled and slid the box toward her in a gesture of sharing. She quickly grabbed a cookie and pulled the box closer to her, to indicate ownership. Moments later the man again took a cookie and returned to his paper. "How rude these Europeans!" she thought, and she again snatched a cookie from the box. The exchange of cookie grabs continued until there was but one cookie left. The woman was in total disbelief when she watched the man take the last cookie, break it in half and leave her but a half of cookie. Several moments later the man's plane was called. He stood up, tipped his hat and bid her good day. Moments later the woman's plane was called. She collected her belongings and when she went to put her book in her carry-on bag, she opened her bag and with shock and embarrassment she saw her unopened box of cookies. She had been eating *his* cookies!

In the absence of reality, clarity and factual information, our minds build assumptions and conclusions about the way things are. Those thoughts then give rise to certain behaviors both subtle and not so subtle.

Self-Conclusions

The *Conversation for Reality and Clarity* also challenges us to suspend conclusions we may hold about ourselves. Let me share an example of a supervisor who was getting stuck because of conclusions he held about himself. I was asked to help a group resolve some sticky issues, resistance and morale problems. The group consisted of approximately twenty equipment operators and their supervisor. I spoke with the supervisor who told me everything he had been doing to get his "guys on board." Much of what he said reflected a sound understanding of management and supervision. He was very current in his reading of management theory and practices. However, after sitting in a couple of his staff meetings, I was able to see the problem. We met in his office and I presented to him what I had observed. "...Your guys are all very seasoned in this work. They know this facility forward and backward. And when you presented the operational problem and asked for ideas, you shot down every idea they offered, and ended up directing them to carryout your idea. You did this several times. Finally, they just sat back and didn't say anything else. Did you notice?" Without answering my question he said, "Well one thing you need to understand, I spent twenty-five years in the Navy. Command and control is what I know. Furthermore, I was raised on the east coast. We're not as laid-back and easy-going as people out here on the west coast. So if these guys don't like it they can find the door." His conclusions about himself were absolving him of any responsibility to be the kind of leader the group needed. Indeed his conclusions were keeping him, his group and his career stuck.

Some examples of self-conclusions include:

> "Of course I have a temper, I'm Italian."
> "I'm just a worker. Management is the one running this show."
> "I don't have a college degree, so I know this is about the best job I can get."

In fact, to this last example, look at how such a conclusion minimizes our own capabilities and potential. I know of a woman who for years operated from the conclusion that she could not change jobs and better herself because she did not have a college education. She suffered the job and spent countless hours complaining about aspects of her job or company, stuck because she discounted her ability to get a better job. She came to understand how that conclusion was restraining her, and she began to simply operate out of her commitment to excellence and organizational results. She spoke with whomever she needed to further the organizations objectives and quality concerns. That woman is now vice-president of operations in a growing manufacturing firm. She has developed tremendous self-confidence in her abilities to influence a company and the lives of its employees in a very positive way. She has, to the greater extent, let go of her limited belief drawn from her conclusion that without a college education she could not get ahead. Her drive, commitment to excellence and personal qualities and strengths were all too visible to her upper-management, who moved her into a position of significant responsibility and influence. Where might a career go if one let go of such limiting conclusions and beliefs?

It also seems to be helpful in the *Conversation for Reality and Clarity* to be clear about what we know and then about what we don't know. Have you heard the expression, "In the absence of solid information people will make it up"? By discussing explicitly the things we don't yet know, it helps block attribution from others. That is, they cannot create some misinterpretation or otherwise invent something, if we have explicitly said "We don't or won't know something until after we complete our analysis and compare the two alternatives. The analysis is supposed to be completed by the 18th, and the Board will compare the two alternatives at its next Board meeting."

In deciding to use the *Conversation for Reality and Clarity*, people are agreeing to trust what others say at face value. They take what others say as truth, as facts. Consider these conversations:

- "Do you want me to stay late and work on it?"
  "No, go ahead and head on home." They said they didn't want you to stay late. Do you trust them, or do you hang around wondering if they would really prefer that you stay?
- "How much did it cost?"
  "It was $80...if you're upset I can take it back."
  "...No, it's okay." They said it was okay. Do you trust them, or do you harbor guilt and maybe resentment, assuming they really didn't want you to buy it?
- "What's the matter?"

"Nothing." They said there is nothing the matter. Do you trust them?

If you operate out of reality and clarity, and don't attribute anything to the other's words, then it becomes the obligation to speak the truth, for people to say what they mean. No mind-reading, just straightforward truth and facts. Another useful prompt is to simply state what you have "noticed". There is nothing to debate or argue about and you are less likely to attribute motives to someone if you speak about your objective observations and self-disclosure. For example, when you simply state, "I've *noticed* that in the past two meetings you and I have been in opposition to each other's suggestions. Would you be willing to explore this with me?" Or, "I have been noticing that I am feeling resistant to the impending merger. I'm not very clear on why I'm feeling that way, but can I discuss it with you?"

Finally, if you operate out of clarity and cannot attribute blame and motives to organizational breakdowns and disappointments, then the organization must look at its breakdowns and disconnects as simply data. The data is then just an indicator that you have not yet created the organization you desire to have, so what do you need to generate or create to become more of the organization you desire to be?

In summary...
Organizations and people can get stuck...
- If they are struggling with an issue or situation, and are attributing motives, intentions and blame to others;
- If they are drawing conclusions and offering opinions about the way things are;
- If they're leaving it to others to guess or make up stories regarding what is not known; and

- If they are operating out of conclusions about themselves that absolve them from responsibility, accountability or otherwise discounts their capabilities.

In those circumstances, a *Conversation for Reality and Clarity* will help get them unstuck.

Chapter 4
The Conversation for Options and Alternatives

This conversation is just what it appears to be, the conversation about what is possible. We are where we are, have what we have because of the way we have approached operations, communications, administration of policies, etc. To continue with the same way of operating will only serve to bring us back to where we are. The *Conversation for Options and Alternatives* considers five elements:

- Brainstorming options and alternatives;
- Pattern breaking;
- Introspection;
- A relentless spirit; and
- Small steps.

In the case of XYZ company discussed earlier, their "do-loop" of training, etc. reinforced and entrenched the notion that each new approach to culture change was "just the flavor of the day."

So organizations have to ask, "Now that we have everyone who needs to be 'on board' committed to the same higher-level results, what are our options? What is possible now that we are clear about what happened, and agree that it makes sense that we are where we are?" The *Conversation for Options and Alternatives* is about brainstorming and generating ideas for possible actions that will help us make some progress toward the results we want to create. Important considerations in this conversation are:

- What's missing?
- What seems impossible, such, that if we had it, it would fundamentally help us make significant progress toward our objectives?
- What are some small steps that will help us make some progress today?
- Are we maintaining a relentless spirit toward our objectives, seeing failures and barriers as just a point to reconnoiter, and ask, "So what's possible now?"

Brainstorming Options And Alternatives

Col. Rolf Smith (Ret.) of the School for Innovation out of Houston Texas would guide groups through "Creative Thinking Expeditions." On one such expedition he coached us to examine the "Seven Levels of Change". That is, when examining your options think about the following:
- Doing things right – try following the procedure;
- Doing the right things – try doing what is truly important;
- Do away with things – stop doing things;
- Doing things better – improve things;
- Doing things others are doing – benchmark best practices;
- Doing things differently – generate novel ideas for doing things;
- Do the impossible – find ways to do things that here-to-fore have been impossible.

Through his guidance in a focused conversation of alternatives and possibilities, an innovative approach for disposing of a hazardous and volatile substance was devised.

Pattern Breaking

The *Conversation for Options and Alternatives* is especially critical to breaking historical and entrenched patterns that may be holding us back. Consider the pattern a manager and one of his senior engineers had for three years:

Pattern #1

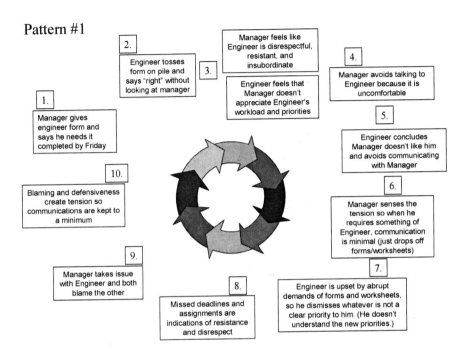

After identifying their pattern, and holding some frank and in-depth discussions as to the higher-level results and impacts it would create if they eliminated their conflicts, they were able to discuss possible ways to intervene in the pattern. A pause, a polite gesture, a request, an invitation for questions or more information, a weekly priorities discussion were all alternatives and possibilities they began to apply, along with some disciplined ego-management. They both demonstrated an earnest commitment to continue working on the relationship and keeping the higher-level results in focus. Over the course of a couple of months they confirmed that they were working much better together.

When we find ourselves in historical patterns that we do not like, and we are not creating the results we want, the first step is to identify the pattern. Sketch it out if necessary. Then examine each step of the pattern and ask, "What are our options and alternatives? What's possible at each point in the pattern, to break or intervene in the pattern?" When workgroups discuss and identify their patterns, they usually can see that everyone in the workgroup can find some possible way to intervene in the pattern. This is true for those who are vocal and emotional, those who remain silent and shut down, supervisors, union stewards and those in other roles.

Another example is offered below. The work group was presented with the pattern. They validated that it was an accurate reflection of their group, and then they entertained the *Conversation for Options and Alternatives* to identify ways to intervene in the pattern.

Pattern #2

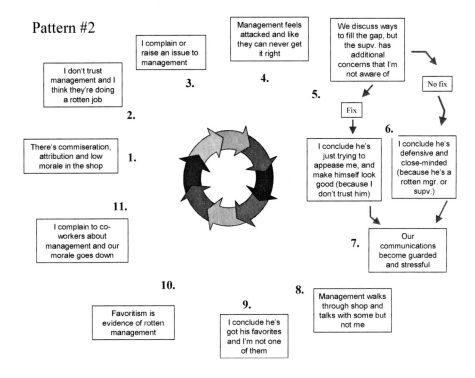

The above pattern was reinforced by some who would join in the complaining and bashing of management. It was also reinforced by some who would just remain silent.

These patterns can be fairly simple or somewhat complex. The key is to identify them and then use the *Conversation for Options and Alternatives* to determine how to intervene when the pattern starts, thus keeping it out of the workgroup. In the above case, the silent people saw the alternative to withdrawing and remaining silent was to speak up and encourage others. The vocal ones saw the possibility of not being the delegated representative of others' complaints, and so on.

It is probably worth mentioning that the more desperate a person is--the more stuck they are--the harder it is for them to entertain options. That's when it is important to seek others' ideas as to options, alternatives and possibilities. People who are desperate and feeling threatened or at risk may fail to see any alternatives or options for themselves sometimes resorting to desperate measures. It is important to help them to have the *Conversation for Options and Alternatives.*

When people begin to identify the possible options and small steps they can initiate today, the pattern begins to shift. Different decisions, different habits, different responses to the old dynamics, all of these begin to create different outcomes. Sometimes I am asked, "What is the likelihood of change if there is only one person trying to break a pattern?" I share with them my recollection of the old science program, Mr. Wizard, from the black and white television era. In one episode Mr. Wizard had a plexi-glass box with a bunch of ping-pong balls in it. He also had a blower attached to the box, and when he turned on the blower the balls began to erratically bounce around within the box. Initially it was chaos. But then after a brief period, the balls began to circle the box in a clearly visible pattern. With the pattern established, Mr. Wizard then inserted a dowel into the box, disrupting the pattern and creating chaos again. However, after another brief period, the balls assumed a pattern. Only this time it was a new and different pattern. The single point of intervention, the single change to the existing pattern created a new pattern. And my own experience supports this result. In a professional sense, when I come in to work with an organization or work group, I am the single point of intervention. By intervening and requiring different actions, communications, and so on, I begin to create a different pattern and new way for the group to operate. As a single point of intervention facing a tremendous historical pattern of habits, communications and routines, I must be steadfast in my efforts to change the pattern. And resistance to change such patterns will come from every level of the organization, even from those who have requested my help. The tyranny of the familiar is a very powerful dynamic. The key to such single point change however, is the determination of the one intervening in the pattern. Obviously, if Mr. Wizard removes the dowel, the pattern will return to its original form. How badly do you want different results, and how committed are you to creating those results? Are you willing to do whatever it takes—subordinating your ego, creating time for dialogue and listening, etc.? You may have to endure a period of chaos before a new pattern emerges.

Introspection

The *Conversation for Options and Alternatives* is both a collective conversation as well as a personal and introspective conversation since in any situation it may serve us to silently consider our options and alternatives.

E.g., This meeting is not going well, I guess I could...

> React emotionally;
> Assert my position;
> Listen;
> Translate their issues to values values;
> Seek the common ground;
> Give in;
> Suggest a recess;
> Pout and be sullen;
> Request another opinion;
> etc.

Case File

A corporate Contract Manager (CM) was required to have all of his contracts over a certain dollar threshold reviewed by a designated attorney. The CM initially found the level of the attorney's scrutiny and the extent of the attorney's required changes to be onerous, time-consuming and beyond reasonableness for what he perceived was the level of contract risk. The CM repeatedly found himself butting heads with the attorney, and arguing defensively for the integrity of the contract as it was prepared, only to leave the attorney's office in defeated exasperation. He entertained the *Conversation for Options and Alternatives*. And he saw an option that proved successful in many ways. He began to bring his contracts in for the attorney's review, saying, "Rick, I'm not too sure about some of these indemnity provisions. Can you give me some guidance there?" He began to operate in deference to the attorney's expertise, with regard, and acting as one being mentored. The change was dramatic. In a period of two months the nature of the relationship had changed. When the CM would bring contracts in for the attorney's review, the attorney would ask, "Anything here give you trouble?" If not, the attorney would sign off, saying something to the effect, "I know your work." Faced with the awareness that his argumentative approach was not getting him the results he wanted, his introspective *Conversation for Options and Alternatives* moved him to an idea that created different results, and changed the very nature of their working relationship.

What options and alternatives are there for creating and generating the kind of organizational relationships and processes you desire within your organization?

Be Relentless
Pursuing options and alternatives to difficult situations offers a high likelihood that you will encounter resistance and barriers.

Some people may find that it is their nature to give up on an objective or goal after encountering barriers once or twice. Ask for it once, encounter resistance. Argue louder and longer, and encounter pushbacks. Some may give up. However, when pursuing important results, the *Conversation for Options and Alternatives* demands that we be relentless. Continuing to seek alternatives, asking others for their ideas, and even examining impossibilities.

Tip: *Ask yourself, "What seems impossible now, but if it could be instituted would significantly enable you to make progress toward your goals?" Then ask, "What would it take to make the impossible, possible?" As with the breaking of patterns, identify the small shifts or simple small actions. These can sometimes offer a glimpse at another pathway.*

Small Steps
I have mentioned several times in this chapter the idea of taking small steps. I commit space to this subject because sometimes in the pursuit of options and alternatives, people seek the big solution and overlook the small steps. I was discussing this with a colleague who confirmed that in the absence of making a small shift, he was literally "Stuck". He was doing some technical climbing up a shear rock face. He had moved up the rock with confidence until he found himself without a next step. He was stuck in the middle of his climb, clinging with finger tips and toes with nowhere to go. After several minutes of examining and exploring the rock for a handhold, he yelled to his partner, "I'm stuck. There's nothing to get a hold of." His partner a few yards down and to the right yelled, "Can you edge to the right a little?" My colleague moved a mere six inches and could then see his next finger hold, and proceeded confidently up the rock. This is how it can be for our organizational and interpersonal challenges. When we're stuck, it may be some very small

shift or small steps that allows us to see our possibilities and path forward.

One important conversation concerning options and alternatives, is the discussion of who is willing to behave differently or do things differently? I have found it useful, albeit somewhat formal, to compile a group's list of possibilities into a Likert-scale assessment that allows each person to self assess against the various possibilities"

1 = "No way I am going to do this."
2 = "I'd like to but don't know how."
3 = "I will if others will."
4 = "I will no matter what."

We then discuss if there are certain possibilities people are just not willing to undertake, and so on for each of the four ratings. The collective discussion seems to give people permission from their peers to do things differently. This has included one pattern-breaking possibility where the work crew had identified that part of their angst and morale problems stemmed from the lack of effective supervision. The possibility was offered that the supervisor step up and supervise. When we discussed what people were willing to begin doing the supervisor stated he was going to step up and supervise, no matter what. He broke through the need to be liked and began giving the crew what they needed and actually wanted.

In summary…
People and organizations can get stuck when:
- They fail to see the higher-level options and possibilities for doing things differently (like those organizations doing the morale surveys, only to find they repeatedly have the same issues);
- They limit their options to things they've done before;
- They give up after encountering resistance or barriers; and

- They fail to see the small steps for making some progress.

And that is when the *Conversation for Options and Alternatives* is needed.

Chapter 5
Conversation For Opportunities

It is generally agreed that the one constant in life is change. And what we know about change is that when things change, we must change with them. However, have you noticed that when people and things are changing, most people first perceive what is wrong with the change and any threats associated with the change? Like Chicken Little they scurry around complaining and warning others that the "sky is falling!" However, among the crowds of those concerned with the negative aspects of change, there is a small percentage of people who examine the change and see the opportunities. The *Conversation for Opportunities* is a small, often silent conversation we can have that directs us constructively toward opportunities that are presented in any given situation. The expression "cooler heads prevail" is representative of people who know how to step back, keep their head above the chaos, the mundane or the shifting, and identify the opportunities to move any of their possibilities and options forward.

The *Conversation for Opportunities* suggests that when I know the results I want (in my business, workgroup, career or job), and I have thought about various possibilities and options for making progress toward what I want, then I can identify, create and leverage my opportunities to move my options forward.

To take advantage of my opportunities, I must be aware of them. All too often people can get caught up in the daily

> **Who sees that they have an opportunity to move any of our possibilities forward?**

routine, fighting today's fires, and running off to the next meeting. In so doing they miss opportunities to move options forward. In fact the meeting they are rushing off to may be an opportunity, if only it is identified as such. By attending to the *Conversation for Opportunities*, we learn that we can examine the things already on our calendar, people we'll be contacting, or simply the things already in our routine and find ways to take advantage of those opportunities. Examples of sources of opportunity can include such things as:

- Meetings
- Appointments
- While at the airport
- When golfing
- At dinner
- When a particular milestone is met
- During the holidays
- The next time it comes up
- During the staff meeting
- When I have my tools out to work on....
- While waiting in the Dr.'s office
- As we drive to...
- When I do my weekly…
- At the upcoming conference
- When the Board convenes

Since we're already doing these things, why not leverage them to move things forward.

The *Conversation for Opportunities* is about identifying and leveraging our opportunities so that we can minimize the things we add to our already busy lives, while ensuring we act on the options we've identified. It also respects the very real fact that not everybody has the same opportunities. Where some see opportunities, others will not.

Good options are sometimes tossed aside by a vocal few that do not see any opportunity that *they* might have to exercise the option. For example, "Well you know there's no budget for that, so you can scratch that idea." So a valuable option may be lost. And so the option of asking for additional resources is discarded and any other people in the group who might have seen an opportunity to ask for resources are now discouraged from doing so. But what if Generative George was thinking, "You know, I'm playing in the company scrambler with Bill Spendworthy this weekend. I'll have an opportunity to pose our ideas to him." The *Conversation for Opportunities* allows us to examine the broader array of our opportunities.

In one organization with whom I worked, it was the maintenance man who helped them improve their organizational communications. How? He saw the opportunity to move the bulletin board from the upstairs conference room to the base of the stairs, while he had his tools out for other work. In moving the bulletin board to an area where there was a high volume of foot traffic, notices and announcements were more readily seen. Several weeks later he was acknowledged by the organization for the opportunity he had leveraged and on the improvements that had resulted. A simple action perhaps, but the opportunity was seen by someone whose official role was not "communication improvement." Left to the Communications Department, the opportunity might have been overlooked.

When you are sitting in the staff meeting and your group leader looks at you and says, "Then we're agreed, we'll have our holiday party on the 10th, and since you did such a great job last year, why don't you take the lead on pulling it together." No one but you knows that you are involved in year-end close-out activities, taking an aerobics class in the evenings, taking your kids to school and then play practice after school for the church, trying to visit your grandfather in the rest home at least once a week, and so on and so on. However, because you are a good employee, you agree to take this on as well, silently wondering where you'll find the time. In the absence of the *Conversation for Opportunities* we have set the stage for you to do a mediocre job of pulling together the party, and because you will take time, focus and energy from other activities, you sub-optimize in those other areas as well. If on the other hand the group leader had asked, "Who has an opportunity to help organize the holiday party for the 10th?" those who have the opportunity could step forward and help produce a better outcome. And you might even see an opportunity to contribute something without being saddled with the whole thing.

In summary…
Organizations and people can get stuck when:
- They fail to identify and leverage their opportunities;
- They simply add more things to their already busy schedules, priorities and lives; and
- They discard options because a vocal few don't see the opportunity.

That is when the *Conversation for Opportunities* can help us get unstuck.

Chapter 6
Conversation for Initiative

The *Conversation for Initiative* is a critical conversation in which we demonstrate our initiative, integrity and accountability. It is that classic conversation of commitment where we say we will do <u>something</u> by <u>a certain time</u>. A colleague of mine used to express it as "count-on-ability", where others can count on you to do just what you said. I will do <u>this</u> by <u>then</u>. Many of the employees I interview fault their management because their manager makes commitments to which there is no follow-up or closure. Despite best intentions, their manager gets consumed by the daily firefights, and last week's commitment slips the manager's mind. The result is an indictment of the manager's integrity. Employees feel justified in their conclusions of, "Yeah, he always says he'll look into it, but nothing ever comes of it. Management doesn't care."

The *Conversation for Initiative* is vital to one's reputation. And in that respect it challenges us to make only those commitments on which we know we will follow-through. It suggests that we not make commitments simply because we believe it is expected of us, or it's the politically correct thing to do. We must know in ourselves that we will do it. This is where the attention to a small step can be very helpful, and can promote that "bias for progress" rather than the "analysis paralysis" that can come with our search for the perfect solution. For example, if a group is discussing their annual holiday party, I can volunteer to pull it together, at which point I may have just taken responsibility for the whole thing. On the other hand, I can commit to the small step of sending a message by the end of the week, soliciting dates when people will be available. I can know within myself that I will deliver on this one small step, and it will help us make progress. It also shows others that they are able to count on me.

So the *Conversation for Initiative* must include an observable behavior and it must include a starting or closure date. Generative George is explicit when he says:

"I will complete the salary survey by the end of the month."

"I will start posting the executive council minutes weekly, starting tomorrow."

"I will develop a draft of the proposal and have it ready for review by the next meeting."

"I will stop my verbal attacks of management immediately."

This by then, observable and with a start or closure date.

Beware of statements such as those of Historical Harry:

"I will *look* into that."

"I'll *try* to communicate better."

"I'll *follow up* on that."

"I'll *do the best I can.*"

These kinds of commitments are not *Conversations of Initiative.* They are only intentions. And while intentions are important, they are not actions.

The *Conversation for Initiative* is specific. It can relate to commitments we make to others or to ourselves. And even if it is a commitment we make to ourselves, it is suggested that we tell someone else about it to increase our accountability. The *Conversation for Initiative* creates accountability.

In summary…

People and organizations can get stuck when:

- They commit to too much;

- They commit because they believe it is expected of them;
- They only commit to the intent;
- They fail to set a start or closure date; and
- There is no accountability established.

That is when the *Conversation for Initiative* is needed.

Chapter 7
The Conversation For Closure

The last of the Six Conversations For Getting Un-Stuck is the *Conversation for Closure*. This is the conversation that helps others get unstuck from some historical or past event or sticking point. It is the conversation that helps them get closure. It is unlike the other conversations since it is purely situational. You cannot initiate this conversation unless the situation requires it. Further, it is not a conversation you can usually request from others, as you will see. Nonetheless it is a very powerful conversation.

Conversations for Closure include such elements as:

- An apology - At this time is an apology more useful than having been right two or three years ago?
- A thank you - Would a simple and sincere "thank you" help move things forward?
- Empathy and acknowledgment - Did we overlook acknowledging them and can we acknowledge them now for what they went through? Can we exercise some empathy for the hurt, frustration, stress, disappointment or whatever they experienced in the situation?
- A pledge of ongoing support - "I'm sorry that happened. That's not the kind of [manager, co-worker, etc.] I want to be. Will you help me make sure that doesn't happen again? If you see it starting to occur, just take me aside and point it out."

Conversations for Closure may be needed when someone refuses to align or support you, regarding the results you are trying to create. For example:

1. A senior engineer (one of your most experienced) has become cynical and disengaged in staff meetings. He no longer puts in the extra time to complete a project in a timely manner. He has also aligned himself with other critics within the work group. His historical sticking point: two years ago he was passed over for a team lead position. Passed over despite the repeated representations that the division was committed to career advancement and promoting from within. The team leader selected over him came from outside the organization.

2. A senior operator (25+ years on the job) has taken to e-mailing critiques of every management decision, copying the customer, subcontractors and oversight agencies. Since he is high on the union list and working in an environment promoting employees rights to identify safety concerns and quality defects, management feels constrained from being able to address the situation. Each time the employee sends out his messages, his management receives inquiries and requests for further justification of their decision. Meetings are required, as well as additional correspondence to the various stakeholders. Management estimates that the reaction and response to each critique may be running $15-20k. His historical sticking point: Over two years ago, the operator would question and banter with his autocratic supervisor, thinking it was competitive discussion or debate ("recreational" was the term he used). At one point his supervisor said, "That's insubordination--three days without pay!"

3. A husband returns home from a three-day out-of-town business trip. He walks into the house only to find his wife in a depressed and withdrawn state. Her sticking point: She tells him that their adult son had stopped over

to the house that afternoon. In her discussions with the son, she was reminded that when the kids were still at home (4 years ago) the husband had always made her the butt of the jokes.

People get stuck for all kinds of reasons. They can reach a point at which they draw a line in the sand. Deciding never to support management's efforts, never to agree to put in any overtime, withdraw support, affection, or whatever. *Conversations for Closure* are about helping people get over their sticking point. They are needed when:

- an old issue resurfaces again and again;
- an old issue gets tied to or is projected on to a current issue (and may be punctuated by stronger emotion than the current issue warrants); or
- there appears no rational reason why they refuse to come into alignment with you regarding your higher-level results and impacts.

When the businessman returned home to find his wife in a down mood, he knew instantly that a *Conversations for Closure* was needed. She was referring to an historical occurrence. He knew his old approach had never worked: "Honey c'mon, get over it, that's ancient history...water under the bridge...geez, have a sense of humor." For some reason persuasion, rationalizing and justifying just didn't liberate her from those old feelings. He had tried that approach for years, and it only resulted in his wife staying tense and upset for hours or even days afterward. Fortunately, he understood the *Conversations for Closure*, which went something like this:

Husband: Honey, what's the matter?

Wife: Oh, Danny was over here this afternoon and we were talking about when the kids were still living here at home. And it just reminded me of how you always made me the butt of the jokes.

Husband: Gosh, that probably felt pretty crummy.

Wife: Yea, it did.

Husband: Well, I'm sorry. (pause) Do I still do that?

Wife: No, not really.

Husband: Honey, I really am sorry, that's not the kind of husband I want to be. If you see me starting to do that, just pull me aside and tell me "Joe, this is what I was talking about." Okay?

Wife: Okay.

With the apology, some empathy and a pledge of support going into the future, his wife was out of her low mood in a matter of a few minutes instead of hours or days. And it is not a manipulation since the two of them are in alignment and agreement as to the kind of marriage and relationship they are trying to create.

In the case of the senior operator who had taken to criticizing management via e-mail every time they made a decision, the call came in from a corporate VP. He explained what was going on, and their concerns of being accused of retaliation if they tried to stop him. When we met later and discussed the situation in greater detail, I agreed to speak with the troublesome employee.

Discussions with the employee at his work location, revealed an intelligent, witty, and authentic man who was "stuck". He was very open and honest about the e-mail campaigns. He told me about when his new supervisor had come on board, and how the new supervisor seemed to have something to prove. He explained how the new supervisor would frequently criticize him for how he was running the plant and would direct him to do things contrary to how Jim had been doing them for years. Jim would take these opportunities to banter back and debate with the supervisor. This was where he termed it "recreational." However, at one point, the supervisor was in no mood for debate and rebuffed Jim, saying, "That's insubordination! Three days without pay!"

Jim went on to explain his sentiments, saying, "You can give me the worst job on this site, and call me every name in the book. But when you take money out of my check, that's food out of my kids' mouths, and that's when it becomes personal. And that's when I started the e-mail thing."

In a subsequent meeting with the VP and his management team we discussed what Jim had shared, and the recommendation for a *Conversation for Closure*. It was explained that Jim was stuck because of something that had happened about a year-and-a half ago, when he got docked three day's pay, and we needed to find a way to get him unstuck. They interrupted saying that Jim was just going to have to get over it, accept it, get on with life and stop the e-mail nonsense. I agreed and told them they ought to have that conversation with Jim. "We have!" the VP responded. "And how has that worked?" I asked. "It hasn't" he replied. We discussed why a *Conversation for Closure* was needed, indicating that it might require an apology, acknowledgment, etc. Jim's Department Manager interrupted, explaining, "We're not about to apologize for docking his pay. We had HR and Legal approval...we even had meetings with the Union! We're not going to go back and reopen that mess!"

"My understanding is that it costs you from $15-20,000 every time you have to respond to one of these e-mail critiques, considering all the meetings, drafting responses to agencies, and not even considering the opportunity costs that are lost. (There was affirmative nodding.) So what's more important at this point, having been right two years ago or getting Jim on board and stopping the nonsense?" After a brief pause, the VP said, "Stopping this e-mailing nonsense."

"Then have a *Conversation for Closure* with Jim" I said. They asked again what that would look like. In discussing what that might look like in this specific instance, we discussed some safety suggestions Jim had made. Since they had even implemented some of them, we discussed giving him a safety award, and a check the equivalent of three day's pay. Their look of astonishment was followed by another round of justification and explanation as to why they had been "right" in docking his pay. Again the question was posed, "But what is important at this time, having been right and keeping his three day's pay, or stopping the e-mailing and the loss of $15-20k every time it happens?" They understood the need to create alignment and allegiance now, and that is what they did. About 20 months later I ran into the VP. I asked him how that issue had settled out. He told me that the e-mails and critiques had stopped as soon as they had held the meeting and returned his three days pay. In fact the VP had even visited the facility where the operator worked to see if the operator was still working for them. He was still there, and no longer stuck on that historical issue.

Conversations for Closure are very powerful, but they are not for those who are weak in their commitment to creating something better. Those who attempt *Conversations for Closure* and don't have that true desire to build the desired outcomes and relationship find themselves stuck. They stay stuck because they follow their attempted apology with explanations as to why they did what they did five years ago, or why they said what they said, why they were right. "Closure" is lost to the explanations, justifications and rationale that follow the apology or the acknowledgment. Truly **the temptation to explain how rational we are** is the slippery slope of this conversation. Don't do it. Don't step into the trap of justifying, rationalizing or explaining.

I have encountered numerous situations where people are stuck on historical issues and need a *Conversation for Closure*. Issues range from those I mentioned here, plus being passed over for promotional opportunities, not being acknowledged for an extended level of effort above and beyond the call of duty, family issues, spousal issues, a pattern of put-downs, etc. In some cases I've had the opportunity and benefit of helping people have their *Conversation for Closure*, and have seen closure of the issue and mending of the relationship occur. In other cases I have observed the conversation fail when the ego steps in, and much higher value is placed on having been right and self-justified in doing whatever caused the offense, rather than getting closure on the issue.

A Note to those who might need closure:
As I mentioned at the start of this chapter, the *Conversation for Closure* is not one you can readily ask for. That is, if you are stuck because of something someone said or did, you may not be able to ask them to have a *Conversation for Closure* with you. So if you are stuck because of this past transgression (perhaps you were passed over for a promotion) the ego is happy to keep you stuck in righteous indignation, and at the cost of your longer-term objectives. But if you want to move forward, which conversation might help? Clearly, the *Conversation for Options and Alternatives* may reveal a number of possibilities for you. Seeking a *Conversation for Reality and Clarity* might give you a clearer understanding of what happened, and allow you to let go of any conclusions or attributions that are keeping you stuck. The *Conversation for Results and Impacts* might allow you to enlist others to help create an organization even better at promoting career development for its employees, and so on.

On the other hand if the trust and communications are healthy enough, you might be able to say, "You, know, that's the third time I've been passed over for a team lead position. And with all of your pledges to 'promote from within,' I've got to say I'm not feeling especially committed to this organization." You can see how this conversation might set up the possibility for an apology, or it might set up rationalization and defensiveness.

It would be nice if we could ask for that *Conversation for Closure* for ourselves whenever we need it, but for now it may be a conversation that we are equipped to give to others. Perhaps in modeling it within the organization, it will cultivate the capability in others.

In summary…
Organizations and people can find themselves stuck if:

- Those they need "on board" with them repeatedly return to a past issues that hold them back;
- They are repeatedly justifying, defending or rationalizing the past to others;
- They find themselves telling others to "get over it" or "that's water under the bridge"; and
- They feel it is more important to have been "right" at that historical point, than to have a constructive relationship now.

That is when a *Conversation for Closure* is a great option to help them get unstuck.

Chapter 8
Summary

Generative thinking and six conversations. It is not a panacea. It is a simple communication construct that can help any organization or individual break out of historical "do-loops" and create different and better outcomes. It boils down to this: Develop your capacity to truly listen and manage your ego, and when you find yourself stuck or recycling through the same old outcomes, ask yourself, "Which conversation do we need to have?"

- The Conversation for Results and Impacts;
- The Conversation for Reality and Clarity;
- The Conversation for Options and Alternatives;
- The Conversation for Opportunities;
- The Conversation for Initiative; or
- The Conversation for Closure.

I have taught the Seven Habits for Highly Effective People, and believe strongly in the validity of those principles. I have taught the modules surrounding the Zenger-Miller basic principles and believe in the validity of those principles. I have read the Rules for Right Living, the 10 Rules for Being Human, and numerous other inspired writings, principle sets and philosophies. These six conversations are not meant as a replacement for any set of principles, philosophy or methods you use to increase your personal effectiveness. They are simply offered as a communication construct that will help you to get "un-stuck" and create the outcomes to which you are committed. If you believe your organization often recycles (putting different meat in the sausage maker only to get the same results) or is otherwise "stuck", apply the communication tenets discussed in this text and create the organization you want.

Things to remember when trying to operate generatively:

1. **The ego doesn't care about your long-term results.** The ego wants to win, look good, be right, avoid embarrassment, avoid being wrong, and it wants these things in the immediate conversation. So in the interest of our long-term results we must suppress or subordinate our ego in the immediate situation. When it wants to defend...listen. When it wants to flee...stay engaged and inquire for clarity and understanding.

2. **Communicate with and engage people in thinking about the longer term, higher-level results.** People may differ over the approach but they can always rally around the results.

3. **Operate with reality and clarity.** Avoid conclusions, opinions, assumptions or attributions. If you assume anything at all, assume that the people you are dealing with are rational people. Even the most cantankerous person is being that way for all of his/her right reasons! We simply don't know the whole story, all of their history or experiences. But if we had perfect knowledge, their behavior would make sense.

4. **Always translate issues, concerns and complaints to values.** Ask yourself, "When I have expressed similar resistance, what is it I am really after? Why would someone care about this (the object of resistance or concern)?" "What are they saying they want more of in our organization?"

5. **Maintain a bias for making progress** (as opposed to perfection). Take satisfaction in taking those small steps that are possible even before the larger actions become viable. Any small step is progress.

6. **Identify and break the patterns** that are not serving you, using the *Conversation for Options and Alternatives.*
7. **Identify and leverage your opportunities and allow others to leverage theirs,** amidst the chaos and the mundane,
8. **Be specific as to what you'll do and by when,** when you commit to take an action.
9. **Help others get complete on historical sticking points, and avoid explaining and rationalizing.**

Months later….

Harry saw George in the cafeteria. "Hey, George, where have you been? I haven't seen you in months," Harry asked.

"Oh, you must not have seen the memo Harry. I was transferred to the new Regional Office to head up the Asia-Pacific operations," replied George.

"Wow, that sounds great George. What an opportunity. How's it going?" inquired Harry.

"Its very exciting," said George. "We've still got a lot of work ahead of us, but we're making progress and building a better operation everyday….So, how are things going for you?"

"Aw, I'm still stuck in the Analysis Group. They'll never throw me any kind of bone. Corporate just hired this new gal as our Group lead, but she's clueless. This place will never change. You know how it is," said Harry. "It's not what you know, it's who you know."

George broke off the conversation, saying, "Harry it's good to see you. I'm sorry I don't have more time, but I need to get into a working lunch with Laura. We're working to see how we can generate a better system for coordinating changes across regions. But Harry, I'd like to talk to you about something I read recently. Give me a call and let's set up a time to have lunch. I think you might find you're not as stuck as you think."

"Really?" said Harry. "That sounds great. I'll give you a call this afternoon."

Later George explained to Harry the concepts and conversations for staying generative and creating desired results. And the rest is history, or perhaps we should say Harry generated a different and better outcome.

Application Assessment

The Application Assessment on the following pages is provided as a follow-up tool, to assist you in checking how you are doing at applying generative thinking, ego management and the *Six Conversations*. It also provides a form of immediate guidance regarding how to apply the concepts and tools in this book. Take a look at it now for ideas, and then take the assessment in 30-60 days, or at least periodically to see how you are doing on application.

The purpose of this assessment is to determine the extent of your own application of the *Six Conversations*. There are no right or wrong answers. The value of the assessment is to see where you have opportunities to apply the Six Conversations to a greater extent, to get the results you want. Read each statement in context of the given situation (within work group, at home, etc.), and then circle the frequency you believe applies.

Results and Impacts

- I stay focused on the higher level results we are working toward when in discussions with others.
  Never..........Rarely..........Sometimes..........Usually..........Always

- I listen to others ideas to determine how they'll work with mine.
  Never..........Rarely..........Sometimes..........Usually..........Always

- I am willing to let go of my ideas or approach for the sake of progress toward our goals.
  Never..........Rarely..........Sometimes..........Usually..........Always

- I remind others that it is not about the approach, but the results that matters most.
  Never..........Rarely..........Sometimes..........Usually..........Always

- I consider or ask, "Who else needs to be on board with us to move things forward?"
  Never..........Rarely..........Sometimes..........Usually..........Always

- I communicate to foster mutuality, or to make sure we are all on the same page.
  Never..........Rarely..........Sometimes..........Usually..........Always

- I ask, "What did you hear me say?"
  Never..........Rarely..........Sometimes..........Usually..........Always

- I ask, "Where do you need additional clarity?"
  Never..........Rarely..........Sometimes..........Usually..........Always

- I ask, "What's missing for you?"
  Never..........Rarely..........Sometimes..........Usually..........Always

- If I don't agree with something someone tells me, I respond by telling them what I heard; where I need additional clarity; and what is missing for me from what they said.
  Never..........Rarely..........Sometimes..........Usually..........Always

- I try to listen and translate issues, concerns and complaints of others to the underlying values those issues represent.
  Never..........Rarely..........Sometimes..........Usually..........Always

- I try to voice my complaints, concerns or issues in terms of the values they represent.
  Never..........Rarely..........Sometimes..........Usually..........Always

Reality and Clarity

- When pursuing objectives or when I meet challenges I seek clarity regarding 'what happened' or just 'what is the true situation.'
- Never..........Rarely..........Sometimes..........Usually..........Always

- I avoid attributing motives or intentions to others.
  Never..........Rarely..........Sometimes..........Usually..........Always

- I avoid offering unfounded conclusions or opinions about the way things are.
  Never..........Rarely..........Sometimes..........Usually..........Always

- I encourage others to remain objective.
  Never..........Rarely..........Sometimes..........Usually..........Always

- I seek facts and objective data about any given situation.
  Never..........Rarely..........Sometimes..........Usually..........Always

- I realize that in any situation we are where we are for all of the right reasons.
  Never..........Rarely..........Sometimes..........Usually..........Always

Options and Alternatives

- In accepting the current state of any situation, I then ask, "So what's possible to move us/me in the right direction?
  Never..........Rarely..........Sometimes..........Usually..........Always

- I exercise a relentless attitude in seeking options when I encounter barriers to something important to me.
  Never..........Rarely..........Sometimes..........Usually..........Always

- I ask others for their ideas regarding possibilities.
  Never..........Rarely..........Sometimes..........Usually..........Always

Options and Alternatives (continued)

- I consider even the smallest possible steps to get unstuck.
  Never.........Rarely.........Sometimes.........Usually.........Always

- I consider the possibilities that pertain to me and my own thoughts and behaviors as it applies to any situation.
  Never.........Rarely.........Sometimes.........Usually.........Always

Opportunities

- I look at where I already have opportunities to move any particular possibility forward.
  Never.........Rarely.........Sometimes.........Usually.........Always

- I listen to the ideas of others and consider my opportunities to support them.
  Never.........Rarely.........Sometimes.........Usually.........Always

- I am aware of my opportunity to move an idea or possibility forward when it arises.
  Never.........Rarely.........Sometimes.........Usually.........Always

- I leverage my current opportunities to promote progress toward our goals.
  Never.........Rarely.........Sometimes.........Usually.........Always

- As opportunities arise I encourage others to help create the results to which we are committed.
  Never.........Rarely.........Sometimes.........Usually.........Always

- I see meetings, milestones, events and interactions with others as opportunities.
  Never.........Rarely.........Sometimes.........Usually.........Always

Initiative

- I exercise the initiative to take very specific actions by specific timeframes or deadlines.
  Never..........Rarely..........Sometimes..........Usually..........Always

- I am aware that others are judging my initiative, integrity and their ability to count on me, when I make commitments.
  Never..........Rarely..........Sometimes..........Usually..........Always

- I know I can count on myself and harbor no self-doubts when I make commitments.
  Never..........Rarely..........Sometimes..........Usually..........Always

- I commit clearly to undertake only the steps I know I can be counted on to take.
  Never..........Rarely..........Sometimes..........Usually..........Always

Constructive Premises

- I exercise tolerance, patience and support as we become more of what we want to become.
  Never..........Rarely..........Sometimes..........Usually..........Always

- I encourage others to be relentless in also staying committed to creating the group (or family, marriage, etc.) we want.
  Never..........Rarely..........Sometimes..........Usually..........Always

- I suppress my ego's need to be right, in the interest of the longer-term objectives and results.
  Never..........Rarely..........Sometimes..........Usually..........Always

Never	Rarely	Sometimes	Usually	Always	Total Score
A x 1	A x 2	A x 3	A x 4	A x 5	C
B	B	B	B	B	

Score the assessment following the instructions on the following page.

Scoring

Conversations for Closure are not included in this "scored" portion of the assessment because the opportunity to have a *Conversation for Closure* may not be readily within your control. They can be situational and vary from person to person.

To score the assessment, total the number of responses in each column, putting the total in box "A" directly below the column. If you had 2 answers in the column marked "never", put a 2 in box "A" below that column. Then multiply that total by the multiplier indicated in the box. Put the product in box "B". Add the box "B" totals together and put the overall score in the large box "C". See the example below.

Never	Rarely	Sometimes	Usually	Always	
2 _{x1}	3 _{x2}	7 _{x3}	22 _{x4}	2 _{x5}	**127**
2	6	21	88	10	

Now continue with the Closure section, and then read how to evaluate your score.

Closure

- I apologize, say 'thank you' or exercise empathy to help others get 'complete' on past hurts or offenses.
  Never..........Rarely..........Sometimes..........Usually..........Always

- I apologize for any part I played in offending them, and <u>not</u> for their 'feeling that way.'
  Never..........Rarely..........Sometimes..........Usually..........Always

Closure (continued)

- When I have apologized I refrain from explaining why something happened or why something was said, and I avoid rationalizing what happened.
Never..........Rarely..........Sometimes..........Usually..........Always

- I keep it foremost in my mind that having a constructive relationship today is worth more than having been right in the past.
Never..........Rarely..........Sometimes..........Usually..........Always

- I offer support by voicing my commitment to building a more constructive relationship or situation now and in the future.
Never..........Rarely..........Sometimes..........Usually..........Always

- When someone brings up a past issue or hurtful situation, I recognize that a conversation for completion is needed to help them get unstuck, and to be in a constructive relationship today.
Never..........Rarely..........Sometimes..........Usually..........Always

Evaluating your score in box C:

A score of 155 or above indicates you are very generative in your approach to work relationships and creating that which is important to you. You are probably viewed as very constructive and optimistic. Examine your possibilities for continuing to cultivate generative conversation within the work group.

A score of 120 – 154 indicates you are primarily generative in your approach toward work relationships and creating that which is important to you. You can assist the work group in its efforts by increasing your focus on any areas where you indicated a "sometimes, rarely or never." Examine your possibilities for asserting yourself more in this regard.

A score of 90 – 119 indicates you are generative in certain situations or relationships. It also indicates you have a tremendous opportunity to become more generative, helping create the work environment you want and more constructive work relationships. Increase your intention to be deliberate about using the Six Conversations. Notice who seems to have a good grasp on the conversations and try to emulate what you see them doing. Be relentless in supporting the use of the Six Conversations.

A score of 89 or less indicates you tend to operate in the historical default. If you are trying to support constructive change within the work group, try to encourage others to join you. Keep the vision of a better work place on your mind and in your discussions. Operate with tolerance, patience, encouragement and support, and view the negatives as evidence that your group is not "there" yet. Increase you personal initiative in trying to use the *Six Conversations*. Consider your possibilities and opportunities for using them. In any given situation ask, "How can we use those Six Conversations here, to get unstuck?"

Note the statements where you indicated "never, rarely or sometimes". These offer specific areas on which you can focus and act. In doing so it will promote progress toward the results you want.

About the Author

Mark Gladstone, lives in the northwest where he is president and principal consultant for the Gladstone Group, Inc. The principles of "Generative Communication" have provided the basis for his work in organizational effectiveness, human-centered change management, team building and conflict management. In conducting his *Six Conversations for Getting Un-stuck* workshops with management teams, organizations and individuals he continues to receive validation of the value of the principles in all areas of relationship management and culture development.

He has over eighteen years of experience helping clients achieve success in their business and personal development. He has acted in the capacity of internal and external consultant, facilitator, trainer, program manager, mediator, mentor and coach. His facilitation and consulting experience includes corporate-wide managed change programs, mergers & acquisitions (both international and domestic), strategic planning, TQM, re-engineering, restructuring and downsizing initiatives. He has extensive experience in personal development, conflict management and team-building, and was an instructor for the Covey Leadership Center's Seven Habits of Highly Effective People. He is an adjunct member of the faculty in Central Washington University's Organization Development Masters program.

In facilitating large-group conferences or interventions, he uses the Six Conversations to accelerate alignment of interests, mitigate resistance, and to quickly translate issues, concerns, and conflict into values.

He received his undergraduate degree in Organizational Communications in 1979, and his Master of Science degree in Organizational Development in 1998.

A Note From the Author

The principle belief underlying my work is derived from the simple phrase, "the power of one." I believe that each of us has the absolute potential to overcome any limitations, to truly make a positive and sustainable difference in whatever areas of life we choose. Throughout history and in everyday life there are incredible examples of people who have committed themselves to making a positive difference, even in the face of tremendous adversity. The organizations that are viewed as the leaders of innovation, cutting edge and pioneering, typically have some single person who has carried the torch through audiences of cynicism and adversity, yet they effectively light the torch for others along the way. It is not a matter of "pumping people up" and creating temporary emotional energy. Rather, it is in helping them recognize their potential, and fostering a steadfast commitment to relentlessly pursue that which they are passionate about, everyday. Coupled with this impassioned belief is a pragmatic understanding that everyone is at a different place along the transformational continuum, and that every organization has a culture and history that moderate the readiness of the people to embrace new visions and ways of doing things. However, without this principle belief in the power of single individuals to make the difference, my own work and sense of contribution would lack meaning and fulfillment.

My modest attempt at sharing the principles of Generative Communications are offered with the hope that they will bolster your capacity to make a difference.

Mark Gladstone

Comments from people who have applied the *Six Conversations for Getting Un-Stuck*:

"Thank you. I am still amazed at the difference this has made to our organization." (6 months out)

"Excellent program. This is really good stuff."

"Thank you. I can't believe what I had settled for. Now I'm creating different results!"

"Thanks for getting us un-stuck!" (60 days out)

"I learned this for the business, but the truth is it has transformed my marriage!"

"This stuff really works!"

For additional copies of this book contact:

The Gladstone Group, Inc. at:

516 S. Wilson
Kennewick, WA 99336
e-mail at: Gladstone-group@charter.net
or call (509) 735-7774.